British History Makers

Alfred the Great

Claire Throp

a Capstone company — publishers for children

Raintree is an imprint of Capstone Global Library Limited, a company incorporated in England and Wales having its registered office at 264 Banbury Road, Oxford, OX2 7DY – Registered company number: 6695582

www.raintree.co.uk
myorders@raintree.co.uk

Text © Capstone Global Library Limited 2017
The moral rights of the proprietor have been asserted.

All rights reserved. No part of this publication may be reproduced in any form or by any means (including photocopying or storing it in any medium by electronic means and whether or not transiently or incidentally to some other use of this publication) without the written permission of the copyright owner, except in accordance with the provisions of the Copyright, Designs and Patents Act 1988 or under the terms of a licence issued by the Copyright Licensing Agency, Saffron House, 6–10 Kirby Street, London EC1N 8TS (www.cla.co.uk). Applications for the copyright owner's written permission should be addressed to the publisher.

Edited by Linda Staniford
Designed by Steve Mead
Original illustrations © Capstone Global Library Limited 2017
Illustrated by Martin Sanders (Beehive Illustration)
Picture research by Ruth Smith
Production by Tori Abraham
Originated by Capstone Global Library
Printed and bound in China

ISBN 978 1 474 73406 6
20 19 18 17 16
10 9 8 7 6 5 4 3 2 1

British Library Cataloguing in Publication Data
A full catalogue record for this book is available from the British Library.

Acknowledgements
We would like to thank the following for permission to reproduce photographs:
Alamy: Anna Stowe, 5, Mary Evans Picture Library, 22, North Wind Picture Archives, cover, Stephen Dorey, 8; Capstone Press: cover, 8; Getty Images: Hulton Archive, 9, Popperfoto, 12; Glow Images: Heritage Images, 24; iStockphoto: Duncan Walker, 16, duncan1890, 21, mona plougmann, 14; Newscom: Fine Art Images Heritage Images, 10, Stapleton Historical Collection Heritage Images, 13, 15, World History Archive, 27; Shutterstock: Aleks Melnik, cover, title page, Awe Inspiring Images, 25, Gregor Buir, cover, background design elements, jorisvo, 23, Khosro, 6, Lian Deng, 11, Paul J Martin, 20, Richard Evans, 17, Toluk, cover, background design elements; Thinkstock: HodagMedia, 4, ProjectB, 26, Hel-hama, 19

We would like to thank Dr Mark Zumbuhl of the University of Oxford for his invaluable help in the preparation of this book.

Every effort has been made to contact copyright holders of material reproduced in this book. Any omissions will be rectified in subsequent printings if notice is given to the publisher.

All the Internet addresses (URLs) given in this book were valid at the time of going to press. However, due to the dynamic nature of the Internet, some addresses may have changed, or sites may have changed or ceased to exist since publication. While the author and publisher regret any inconvenience this may cause readers, no responsibility for any such changes can be accepted by either the author or the publisher.

Some words are shown in bold, **like this**. You can find out what they mean by looking in the glossary.

Contents

Alfred's life 4
History 6
Early life 8
Fighting the Vikings.................................12
More Viking attacks 14
Peace 16
Danelaw 18
Defence 20
Education and law 22
King of the English? 24
Legacy...26

Timeline 28
Glossary 30
Find out more 31
Index 32

Alfred's life

King Alfred is one of the best-known kings in the history of Britain. He was the king who fought and beat the Vikings in the late AD 800s. He formed England's first navy and organized the army. He also tried to improve education and make the law fairer.

FACT

Alfred is the only English king or queen who is known as "Great".

History

In the late AD 700s, people came from Denmark, Norway and Sweden to attack Britain. These people were the Vikings. Britain was divided into different **kingdoms** at the time. The kingdoms spent a lot of time fighting each other. This meant there was no united army to stop the Viking attacks.

This map shows where the Vikings came from and which parts of Britain and Ireland they settled in.

Early life

Alfred was born in AD 849. He had four elder brothers and one elder sister. Alfred spent his childhood travelling around the kingdom of Wessex with his parents. He went to church and enjoyed listening to poetry.

When Alfred visited Rome, he met Pope Leo IV.

FACT

Alfred went to Rome in Italy twice as a child. He first travelled there in AD 853. In 855, after his mother's death, he went again with his father, King Ethelwulf.

Alfred's mother, Osburh, promised to give a book of poetry to the first of her sons to learn it. Books were **rare** at the time. They had to be written by hand, so they were expensive to make. It was Alfred, the youngest son, who learnt the poems first.

This is a page of a book from Alfred's time.

∽ FACT ∽

We know about Alfred's life because a **monk** called Asser wrote about it in AD 893.

This is St David's Cathedral in Wales. Asser was a monk at St David's.

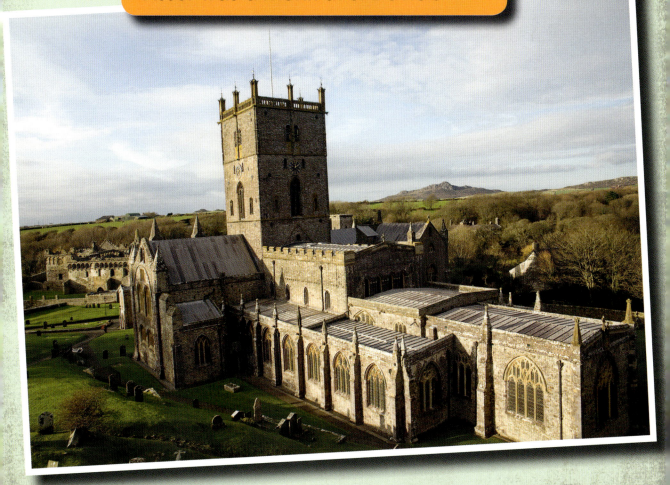

Fighting the Vikings

In AD 868, Alfred married Ealhswith of Mercia. Two years later, the Vikings attacked Wessex. It was the only **Anglo-Saxon** kingdom that had not fallen to the Vikings. Alfred joined King Ethelred, his brother, to fight against the Vikings. They won the Battle of Ashdown in AD 871. But they lost other battles. Shortly after Easter, Ethelred died and Alfred became king.

FACT

Alfred led the fighting at the Battle of Ashdown because Ethelred was at church.

More Viking attacks

In AD 876, the Vikings invaded Wessex again. They nearly captured Alfred in a surprise attack on Chippenham in January 878. Alfred managed to escape into the **marshland** of Athelney. He had to rely on local people for food and shelter.

Villages in Alfred's time would have looked like this.

FACT

There is a famous story from this time. While Alfred was hiding, a woman asked him to watch some cakes she was baking. He let them burn and she was angry with him. The story probably isn't true.

Peace

By spring 878, Alfred had raised an army. They defeated the Vikings at the Battle of Edington in Wiltshire. The army pushed the Vikings back to Chippenham. They **besieged** the town for three weeks. Guthrum, the Viking leader, finally agreed to peace.

King Alfred's Tower marks the place where Alfred rallied his men before the Battle of Edington.

FACT

Unlike many kings, Alfred treated the defeated army's leader well. He threw a 12-day feast for Guthrum!

Danelaw

In AD 886, Alfred made an agreement with King Guthrum to divide England. The Vikings controlled the north and east. This later became known as the Danelaw. Wessex gained land from Mercia and Kent. The Danelaw meant that the Anglo-Saxons and the Vikings were able to live peacefully for a few years.

FACT
In AD 886, Alfred took control of London from the Vikings.

Defence

To guard against further Viking attacks, Alfred improved defences around his kingdom. He built burhs, which were **fortified** towns. He also organized an army and created England's first navy. Many fast ships were built to defend the coast.

Chichester was one of the first burhs Alfred built.

FACT

In AD 890, Alfred supposedly disguised himself as an entertainer. He then went into the Vikings' camp to find out what their plans were.

Education and law

Alfred set up a school for his own children and the sons of leading **nobles**. He brought **scholars** to England from Europe. Books written in **Latin** were now written in English too. Alfred wanted people to be able to read English. Alfred also made the laws of the country fairer.

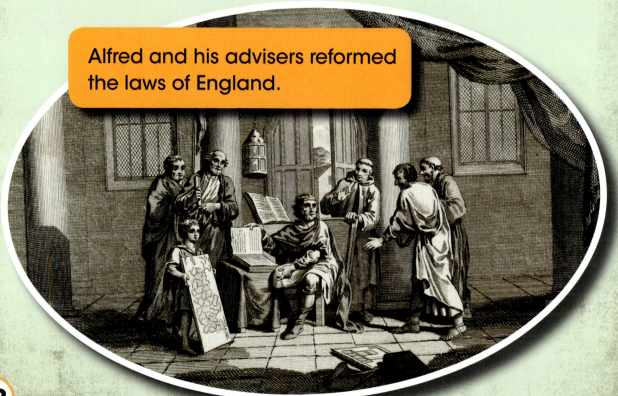

Alfred and his advisers reformed the laws of England.

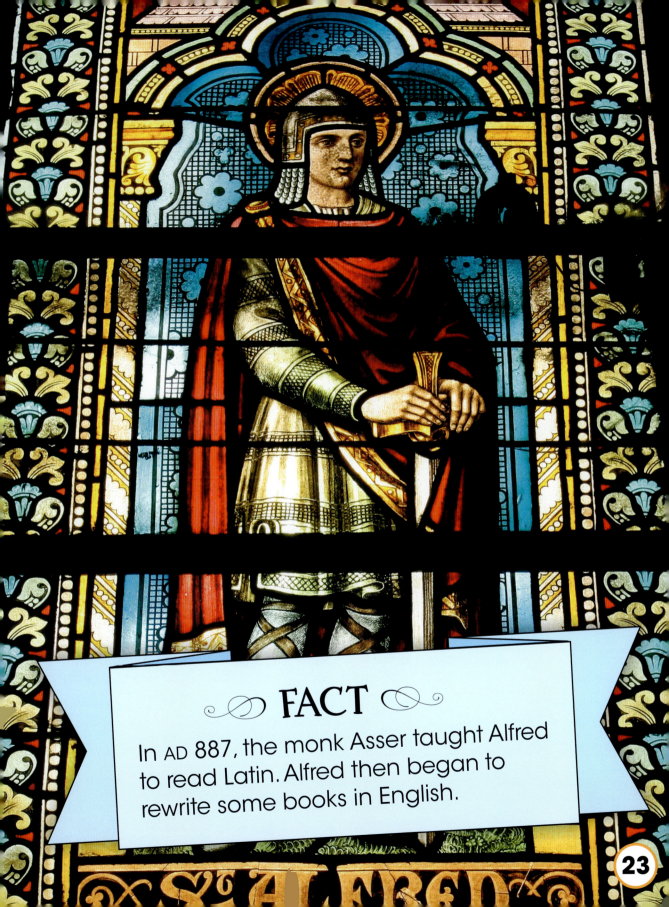

FACT

In AD 887, the monk Asser taught Alfred to read Latin. Alfred then began to rewrite some books in English.

King of the English?

In AD 892, the Vikings attacked again. Alfred's defences held firm. The Vikings left in AD 896. Alfred was able to rule peacefully and continue with his **reforms**.

Alfred died in October 899. He was buried at Winchester Old Minster.

FACT

In the AD 890s, Alfred began to be known as king of the Anglo-Saxons. Some coins described Alfred as "king of the English".

Legacy

King Alfred helped to save the Anglo-Saxons from the Vikings. He was seen as a strong and fair ruler. This helped him to bring together the kingdoms of England. He was able to begin reconquering land held by the Vikings.

～ FACT ～

The Alfred Jewel has the words "Alfred ordered me to be made" around its edge. It may have been a pointer or part of a bookmark.

Timeline

787 First Viking attacks on England

849 Alfred born to Ethelwulf and Osburh

868 Alfred marries Ealhswith of Mercia

870 Vikings attack Wessex

871 Battle of Ashdown; Alfred becomes king

878 Vikings attack Chippenham; Alfred escapes

878 Battle of Edington

886 Land divided between Alfred and the Vikings. This becomes known as the Danelaw.

887 Alfred learns Latin in order to teach others the language too

890s Coins mention Alfred as "king of the English"

892 The Vikings attack again and are defeated

893 Asser writes *Life of King Alfred*

899 Alfred dies in October and is buried at Winchester

Glossary

Anglo-Saxons people who lived in England from the AD 400s. They originally came from areas around modern-day Germany and the Netherlands.

besiege surround a city or town with armed forces in order to gain control of the town

fortified having had walls built for protection from attack

kingdom area ruled by a king or queen

Latin ancient Roman language used by educated people in Anglo-Saxon times

marshland area of low land that is often flooded

monk man who lives in a religious community and promises to devote his life to his religion

noble wealthy person of high rank or birth

rare not often seen, found or happening

reforms changes made to improve something, such as education

scholar well-educated person

Find out more

Books
Alfred the Great and the Anglo-Saxons (History Starting Points), David Gill (Franklin Watts, 2016)
Anglo-Saxons (Fact Cat), Izzi Howell (Wayland, 2015)
Early Kings of England, J M Sertori (Collins, 2016)

Websites
anglosaxondiscovery.ashmolean.org/kings/kings_index.html
This website has lots of information about the Anglo-Saxons and King Alfred.

www.bbc.co.uk/schools/primaryhistory/anglo_saxons
Find out about the Anglo-Saxons on this website.

www.teachinghistory100.org/browse/theme/all/from/3/date/2
Have a look at some Viking and Anglo-Saxon objects to learn more about the time.

Places to visit
Ashmolean Museum
Beaumont Street, Oxford OX1 2PH
Visit this museum to see the famous Alfred Jewel.

Winchester
You can take a city walk to see places connected to King Alfred.

Index

Alfred the Great, 4, 8, 12, 14, 16, 18, 20, 22, 24, 28–29
   childhood, 8–9
   death, 24, 29
   family, 8–9
   story of burning the cakes, 15

Asser, 11, 23, 29

Battle of Ashdown, AD 871, 12, 28
Battle of Edington, AD 878, 16, 28
books, 10, 22, 23

Chippenham, 14, 16, 28

Danelaw, 18, 29
   defences, 20, 24

Ealhswith of Mercia (Alfred's wife), 12, 28
Ethelred (Alfred's brother), 12

Ethelwulf (Alfred's father), 9, 28

Guthrum, Viking leader, 16, 18

laws, 22
London, 18

Osburh (Alfred's mother), 10, 28

schools, 22

Vikings, 4, 6–7, 12, 14, 16, 20, 21, 24, 26, 28–29